W9-AVY-999

THE ELECTORAL COLLEGE

THE ELECTORAL COLLEGE

CHRISTOPHER HENRY

A FIRST BOOK

FRANKLIN WATTS
A Division of Grolier Publishing
New York London Hong Kong Sydney
Danbury, Connecticut

For Paul O'Dwyer, Esq.—in the hearts of his friends forever.

Oh for the swords of former time!
 Oh for the men who bore them,
When, armed for Right, they stood sublime,
 And tyrants crouched before them!

—from Thomas Moore's "Oh For the Swords of Former Time!"

Cover photographs copyright ©: Courtesy, Architect of the Capitol (painting by Howard Chandler Christy); AP/Wide World Photos (inset).

Photographs copyright ©: North Wind Picture Archives: pp. 8, 12, 16 right, 36; The Bettmann Archive: pp. 10, 18, 20, 26, 33 top left, 33 bottom right, 49, 56; UPI/Bettmann: pp. 24, 44; Courtesy, Architect of the Capitol: p. 13 (painting by Howard Chandler Christy); The Library of Congress: pp. 16 left, 17 left, 27, 34 left, 34 right, 54; State Department of Archives and History, Raleigh, N.C.: p. 17 right; The Gamma Liaison Network: pp. 22 (Brad Markel), 38 (Diane Walker), 52 (Alan Weiner); AP/Wide World Photos: pp. 29, 41, 44 inset, 46, 56 inset.

Author photograph copyright ©: Jane Jesse Cardinale

Library of Congress Cataloging-in-Publication Data

Henry, Christopher.
    The electoral college / Christopher Henry.
        p. cm. — (A First book)
    Includes bibliographical references and index.
    Summary: Examines the way in which the electoral college selects the president, indicates drawbacks of the system, and discusses elections in which the electoral winners lost the popular vote.
    ISBN 0–531–20218–6
    1. Electoral college—United States—Juvenile literature. 2. Presidents—United States—Election—Juvenile literature. [1. Electoral college. 2. Presidents.]
    I. Title. II. Series.
JK529.H46 1996   95–43847
324.6'3'0973—dc20   CIP
                                                             AC

CONTENTS

The Electoral College

In 1787, delegates to the Constitutional Convention met to create a document of basic laws and principles for the new country.

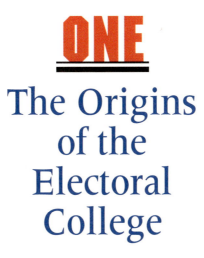

The Origins
of the
Electoral
College

The long, hot summer of 1787 was a time of great conflict for the delegates to the Constitutional Convention in Philadelphia. Although they had declared their independence from England more than a decade earlier, the former British colonies still were searching for a workable system of government. The job of the Constitutional Convention was, in effect, to invent a new kind of national government, one that never had been tried in any other country.

It was no easy task. The summer was filled with

The debate and deal making of the Constitutional Convention of 1787 took place at Philadelphia's State House.

long debates about a wide variety of political issues. If the convention was to succeed, the delegates would have to work out compromises on the most troublesome issues.

One of the biggest conflicts at the convention was over the system of representation to the country's new Congress. There were two plans under consideration. The first proposal, the Virginia Plan, allowed each state a number of congressional representatives based on the state's population. The second proposal, the New Jersey Plan, granted all states, large or small, the same number of representatives. The convention was deadlocked for much of the summer, until a third plan was devised: Congress would be made up of two houses—one with representation based on each state's population, and the other with equal representation for all states.

The long and bitter debate over representation wore out the delegates to the Constitutional Convention. When it came time to face the next tough question—how to elect the president—they seemed determined to reach agreement quickly.

The Constitutional Convention had two choices. It could provide for direct election of the president by the people, or it could give Congress the power to vote for and appoint the president. Early in the summer, the convention leaned toward congressional election of the president. Some delegates, however, objected to a system that would give Congress so much power. They argued that, under a congressional election system, the president would be indebted to Congress for his or her job.

On the other hand, direct election of the president by the people posed problems, too. Some delegates questioned whether ordinary people would know enough about the candidates to make informed choices. Also, having recently declared independence from a king in Britain, the delegates were concerned that a president chosen by the masses might become too powerful.

After a long summer of negotiation, delegates from
twelve states signed the U.S. Constitution on
September 17, 1787.

Once again, the Constitutional Convention reached a settlement. The framers of the U.S. Constitution agreed on an indirect method of electing the president. Instead of a direct vote, voters would select representatives called **electors** to represent their state in a group of electors called the **electoral college.** Each state would have as many electors as it had representatives in Congress. The president would be chosen by the electoral college. The presidential election plan that the convention agreed upon in the summer of 1787 is still in operation today, with some alterations.

As the framers established originally in the Constitution, the electors did not vote for a president and a vice president separately. Electors simply voted for two candidates, without specifying what office they would hold. (Electors were not permitted to vote for more than one person from their own state.) The candidate with the greatest number of **electoral votes** would become president, as long as that candidate won a number of votes equal to a **majority** (more than 50 percent) of the total number of electors.

For example, if there were one hundred electors casting votes for two candidates, two hundred votes would be cast. A candidate would have to receive the votes of a majority of the one hundred electors—at least fifty-one votes—to win the presidency. The candidate with the second-greatest number of votes would be vice president.

In the event that no candidate was selected by the majority of electors, or if there was a tie vote for first place, the House of Representatives would elect the new president. For this vote, instead of each representative, each state would cast a vote. This system gave the smaller states as much power and influence as the larger states.

The system's shortcomings were soon apparent. In the 1800 election, Thomas Jefferson ran for president with Aaron Burr as his vice president. Both men were members of the emerging Democratic-Republican party. Running against them were John Adams and Charles C. Pinckney of the Federalist party. Political parties were a new idea, and it was the first time two parties each had put forward a pair of candidates, or a "ticket," for the nation's two highest offices. Jefferson and Burr each received seventy-three electoral votes; Adams and Pinckney finished third and fourth.

These results threw the American political scene into crisis. The framers of the Constitution had not

Thomas Jefferson and Aaron Burr

considered the possibility that two candidates from the same party would run together as a ticket and receive the same number of electoral votes.

According to the Constitution, the House of Representatives had to settle the election. Neither party, however, commanded a majority in the House. After six days and thirty-five ballots, the House was still deadlocked. Finally, one representative changed his vote, making Jefferson the president. Aaron Burr became his vice president.

To rule out similar crises in the future, Congress passed the Twelfth Amendment in 1804. This amendment provided that in all future elections, the electors would cast two distinct ballots: one for president and one for vice president. Further, the amendment specified that if no candidate for president received a major-

John Adams and Charles C. Pinckney

Congress modified Article II of the Constitution to help prevent presidential elections without a clear winner.

ity of electoral votes, the House of Representatives would choose the president from among the three top electoral vote-getters. As before, instead of each representative, each state would cast one vote.

If no candidate for vice president received a majority of electoral votes, the Senate would elect the vice president from among the two top vote-getters, with each senator casting one vote. Curiously, the Twelfth Amendment made another provision—that neither the House nor the Senate could make its selection without a two-thirds **quorum**, the minimum number of legislators that must be present to enact a law or to conduct other official business. Thus, the amendment left open the possibility that a **minority** of legislators could block the will of the majority by refusing to participate in the proceedings.

The requirement that the Senate choose the vice president from among the two top electoral vote-getters almost assured that one vice presidential candidate would win a majority and serve as vice president. In the event that the country ever was divided between three presidential candidates and the House of Representatives was unable to agree upon a leader, there would be a vice president to lead the country until a new president was chosen.

The authors of the Constitution seem to have presumed that members of the electoral college would act as individual, public-spirited citizens and choose the best candidates. Presidential politics, however, took an unexpected path. The emerging Federalist and Democratic-Republican parties became stronger. Electors in the electoral college began identifying with one or the other party. Instead of functioning as independent citizens, as the framers anticipated, electors began voting in groups, or **blocs**, along party lines. When a party put forward a pair of candidates for president

Congress counts the electoral vote in this sketch from the 1800s. After the first presidential elections, these votes split increasingly along party lines.

and vice president, it became assumed that electors of that party would support those candidates.

This development had one very important consequence. Because electors were voting in blocs, it became more likely that one candidate would emerge from the electoral college balloting with a clear majority. The electoral college would serve less as a preliminary election than as the final point of decision in most presidential elections.

Other changes on the political landscape would mean still more change for the electoral college system.

Casting a ballot in the voting booth is just one part
of the process of choosing a president.

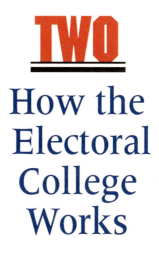

TWO

How the Electoral College Works

When a U.S. citizen enters the voting booth on election day, he or she casts votes for candidates for many offices. In most elections, including those for seats in Congress and state legislatures, the candidate who receives a majority of the vote wins. Sometimes, a candidate wins a **plurality** (50 percent or less of the vote but more than that of any other candidate) and a **runoff election** between the two highest vote-getters might take place. In presidential elections, however, voters do not choose their leaders through a

DIRECTIONS FOR VOTING ON THE VOTING MACHINE

PULL the red handle of the curtain lever (throw left side of the machine) from the left to right as far as it will go and leave it there (this will close the curtain around you and unlock the machine for voting).

On the ballot shown at the right you will find (in column A, column B, column C, etc.) the names of the candidates. Turn down the pointer at the right of the candidate or candidates you wish to vote for until an ⬛ mark appears at the right of each candidate's name for whom you intend to vote, and leave the ⬛ mark showing, from

this

John Doe

to this

John Doe

Leaving the pointer or pointers down in their voting position, pull the red handle of the curtain lever to the left as far as it will go and leave it there (this will register your vote and return the pointers to their first position, after which the curtain will open).

A FEW WORDS OF EXPLANATION

No votes are registered until you pull the curtain lever to its left to open the curtain. You can therefore make as many changes in your ballot as you wish while the curtain lever is at its extreme right (curtain closed).

Each candidate's voting pointer is to the right of his name.

The machine is so arranged that you cannot turn down more than the proper number of pointers for an office. For example, if only one candidate is to be elected for any office you can turn down only one pointer for that office. If more than one candidate is to be elected to an office you can turn down only the number of pointers for the number of candidates to be elected. No vote will be registered for any candidate except that with a pointer left down over his name. So be sure to leave the ...

	Office	Republican A	Democratic B	Conservative C	Liberal D	Socialist Worker E
1	ELECTORS OF PRESIDENT AND VICE-PRESIDENT — Vote once	Richard M. Nixon / Spiro T. Agnew (1A)	George McGovern / R. Sargent Shriver (1B)	Richard M. Nixon / Spiro T. Agnew (1C)	George McGovern / R. Sargent Shriver (1D)	Evelyn Reed / Clifton DeBerry (1E)
2	ASSOCIATE JUDGE OF THE COURT OF APPEALS — Vote for any three	Domenick L. Gabrielli (2A)	Bernard S. Meyer (2B)	Domenick L. Gabrielli (2C)	Bernard S. Meyer (2D)	
3		Hugh R. Jones (3A)	Nanette Dembitz (3B)	Hugh R. Jones (3C)	M. Henry Martuscello (3D)	
4		Sol Wachtler (4A)	Lawrence H. Cooke (4B)	Lawrence H. Cooke (4C)	Sol Wachtler (4D)	
5	JUSTICES OF THE SUPREME COURT 1st JUDICIAL DISTRICT — Vote for any seven	Irving Kirschenbaum (5A)	Joseph P. Sullivan (5B)	Joseph P. Sullivan (5C)	Michael J. Dontzin (5D)	
6		William J. Drohan (6A)	Herbert B. Evans (6B)	William J. Drohan (6C)	Herbert B. Evans (6D)	
7		Alfred H. Adler (7A)	Alvin F. Klein (7B)	Alvin F. Klein (7C)	Murray Koenig (7D)	
8		George C. Mantzoros (8A)	Martin Evans (8B)	Martin Evans (8C)	Harry T. Nusbaum (8D)	
9		Burton B. Roberts (9A)	Burton B. Roberts (9B)	Burton B. Roberts (9C)	Burton B. Roberts (9D)	
10		Joseph A. Macchia (10A)	Martin B. Stecher (10B)	Sidney Eisenberg (10C)	Louis Schifrin (10D)	
11		Thomas C. Chimera (11A)	Thomas C. Chimera (11B)	Thomas C. Chimera (11C)	Thomas C. Chimera (11D)	
12	JUDGES OF THE CIVIL COURT OF THE CITY OF NEW YORK — Vote for any three	Andrew L. Aubry (12A)	Sheldon S. Levy (12B)	Andrew L. Aubry (12C)	David Stadtmauer (12D)	
13		David H. Edwards Jr. (13A)	David H. Edwards Jr. (13B)	Edward J. Schultz (13C)	David H. Edwards Jr. (13D)	
14		Hortense W. Gabel (14A)	Hortense W. Gabel (14B)	Richard Heller (14C)	Hortense W. Gabel (14D)	
15	REPRESENTATIVE in CONGRESS 18th DISTRICT — Vote for one	Jane Pickens Langley (15A)	Edward I. Koch (15B)	Jane Pickens Langley (15C)	Edward I. Koch (15D)	Rebecca Finch (15E)
16	JUDGE OF THE CIVIL COURT 2nd DISTRICT — Vote for one	Olga Kupchin (16A)	Stanley P. Danzig (16B)	NO CANDIDATE	Alfred Toker (16D)	
17	STATE SENATOR 25th DISTRICT — Vote for one	John W. Graci (17A)	Paul P. E. Bookson (17B)	John W. Graci (17C)	Charles Sanchez (17D)	
18	MEMBER OF ASSEMBLY 63rd DISTRICT — Vote for one	Sophie E. Czechlewski (18A)	Anthony G. DiFalco (18B)	NO CANDIDATE	Anthony G. DiFalco (18D)	

When citizens cast a vote for president, they are actually voting for the "electors of president and vice president." This is a New York City ballot from the 1972 election.

direct, **popular vote**. The process of electing a president and vice president is far more complex.

When a voter casts a ballot for a presidential ticket, he or she does not vote directly for the president and vice president. Instead, that voter casts a ballot for a list of electors put forward by each political party, usually the Republicans and the Democrats. That list, or **slate**, of proposed electors has pledged to vote for its party's presidential ticket. In most states, the party slate that wins the most popular votes—votes actually cast by individuals in the voting booth—becomes that state's official electors.

In each state, party committees or conventions usually choose their party's candidates for electors. Independent candidates for president usually are permitted to name their own electors.

The Constitution allows each state a number of electors that is equal to the state's representation in Congress. Each state, then, has one elector for each of its two U.S. senators and one elector for each of its members in the House of Representatives.

The Constitution also requires that a national census, or official population count, be taken every ten years to determine the population of each state. As the states gain or lose population, they gain or lose electors in the electoral college, as well as members of the House of Representatives.

In today's electoral college, there are a total of 538 electors. The electoral college has as many electors as

DISTICTS	Free white Males of 16 years and upwards, including heads of families.	Free white Males under fixteen years.	Free white Females, including heads of families.	All other free perfons.	Slaves.	Total.
Vermont	22435	22328	40505	255	16	85539
N. Hampfhire	36086	34851	70160	630	158	141885
Maine	24384	24748	46870	538	NONE	96540
Maffachufetts	95453	87289	190582	5463	NONE	378787
Rhode Ifland	16019	15799	32652	3407	948	68825
Connecticut	60523	54403	117448	2808	2764	237946
New York	83700	78122	152320	4654	21324	340120
New Jerfey	45251	41416	83287	2762	11423	184139
Pennfylvania	110788	106948	206363	6537	3737	434373
Delaware	11783	12143	22384	3899	8887	59094
Maryland	55915	51339	101395	8043	103036	319728
Virginia	110936	116135	215046	12866	292627	747610
Kentucky	15154	17057	28922	114	12430	73677
N. Carolina	69988	77506	140710	4975	100572	393751
S. Carolina	35576	37722	66880	1801	107094	249073
Georgia	13103	14044	25739	398	29264	82548
	807094	791850	1541263	59150	694280	3893635

The first U.S. census, shown here, was taken in 1790.

Over the centuries, information gathered by census takers
has determined the number of each state's representatives
in Congress and electors in the electoral college.

there are seats in Congress plus Washington, D.C.'s three votes, which were granted in 1961. Currently, the Senate has 100 members (two from each state) and the House of Representatives has 435 members.

The Constitution also gives each state the freedom to decide for itself how electors will be selected to represent the state in the electoral college. In elections of earlier times, the methods varied greatly. In some states, the people chose which party's electors went to the electoral college in a direct, popular vote. In other states, the state legislature chose those electors. Over time, more and more states came to favor direct selection by the people. By the end of the Civil War, in 1865, all states chose electors by popular vote.

Just as the states came to favor popular selection of electors, they gradually adopted a "winner take all" electoral college system. That is, the candidate (or the slate of electors pledged to that candidate) receiving the most votes wins all of the state's electoral votes. Almost all of the fifty states now operate under the "winner take all" system. The two exceptions, Maine and Nebraska, allow their electoral votes to be divided among candidates. These two states together, however, control only nine electors.

As long as it does not violate the provisions of the Constitution, each state is free to choose how to con-

After the general election, electors from all across the country meet in their state capitals to carry out the official act of casting electoral votes.

How the Electoral College Works

On the Tuesday that follows the first Monday in November in an election year:

Voters cast ballots for electors who represent a particular party in each state

On the Monday that follows the second Wednesday in December:

Electors of the party that won the most votes in each state meet in the state capitals to cast ballots for president and vice president

On January 6:

Congress officially counts the ballots cast by electors

On January 20:

The candidate who wins the majority of electoral votes becomes president of the United States

duct presidential elections. Most state laws do not even specifically require that their electors vote according to the will of the people as it is expressed in the presidential election. Some states have such a requirement, but they impose no penalties on electors who violate it. Only five states have laws that penalize electors who violate their pledges to vote for their party's candidates.

However, in practice, it is almost unheard of for an elector not to vote as he or she pledges before the election. Electors are usually longtime party **activists** who would never consider an act of party disloyalty. In fact, fewer than one elector out of one thousand ever has violated a pledge.

More than a month after voters nationwide have exited the voting booths, the winning slates of electors meet in their states to cast ballots for president and vice president. The Constitution requires that, to be elected to either office, a candidate must receive a majority of the total number of 538 electoral votes. Today, a candidate needs 270 electoral votes to win the presidency or vice presidency. Clearly, at this point in the electoral college system, the election already has been decided. The electoral voting is essentially a ceremony, more a formality than a pivotal event in presidential elections.

THREE

Winning the Vote, Losing the White House

After learning how the electoral system works, it should come as no surprise that the candidate who receives the highest number of popular votes— votes cast by individual voters—does not always win the election and become president. Three times in U.S. history, the candidate who received the highest number of popular votes was not elected president.

The first time the popular-vote winner failed to win the presidency was in 1824. In this election, all four candidates were Democratic-Republicans. One

of these office seekers was
Andrew Jackson, a U.S.
senator and soldier who
had joined the South Car-
olina militia at the age of
thirteen to fight in the Rev-
olutionary War. Jackson won
155,872 votes. His nearest rival,
John Quincy Adams of Massachusetts, won 105,321 votes.

None of the four candidates received a majority of the 261 electoral
college votes. With 99, Jackson held
the most electoral votes. Adams
had 84, William H. Crawford had
41, and Henry Clay had 37. As
dictated by the Constitution, in
cases where no candidate has a
majority, the election goes to the
House of Representatives to be

John Quincy Adams

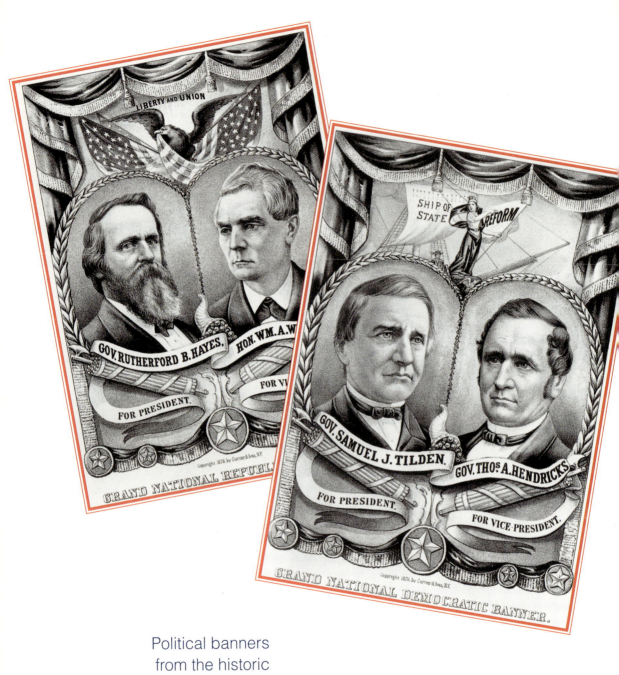

Political banners
from the historic
1876 election

decided. The House voted Adams the nation's sixth president, despite the fact that more Americans had voted for Jackson.

The second time the popular-vote winner failed to win the presidency was in 1876. Republican Rutherford B. Hayes was elected president by the thinnest possible margin. It remains the most controversial election in American history. The votes of several southern states were disputed and Congress appointed a special electoral commission to resolve the predicament. The commission declared Hayes the winner with 185 electoral votes. His Democratic opponent, Samuel J. Tilden, with 184 electoral votes, lost by a single electoral vote. Tilden, however, had led in the popular vote by more than a quarter of a million votes. He had 4,284,757 votes to Hayes's 4,033,950. Nevertheless, Hayes went to the White House and Tilden returned home.

The third time the popular-vote winner failed to win the presidency was in 1888. Republican Benjamin Harrison was elected president with 5,444,337 votes. Like Hayes, Harrison left an angry Democratic opponent, Grover Cleveland, in his wake. Cleveland had received almost 100,000 more votes than his rival. Harrison, however, with sixty-five more electoral votes than Cleveland, was elected.

Although Grover Cleveland won more popular votes in the 1888 presidential election, Benjamin Harrison was inaugurated the twenty-third president of the United States.

That election was the last time that a candidate with the highest popular-vote total was denied the White House. However, over one sixteen-year period, from 1960 to 1976, such an outcome could easily have been the result in two out of five presidential elections.

In 1960, when John F. Kennedy was elected president, his popular-vote margin was less than 120,000 votes out of more than 68 million cast. Kennedy's margin of victory was less than two-tenths of 1 percent. Kennedy won 303 electoral votes to Richard M. Nixon's 219, an 84-vote margin. Nixon trailed Kennedy in Delaware, Illinois, Missouri, Nevada, New Jersey, and New Mexico by only about 50,000 votes. Kennedy beat Nixon in Hawaii by only 115 votes. If Nixon had carried these states, he could have won the presidency without winning the popular election.

In 1976, Democrat Jimmy Carter of Georgia ran against the sitting president, Gerald R. Ford. Ford was the first president in the nation's history never to have been elected to the office of either president or vice president. Ford was a member of the House of Representatives from Michigan when Richard Nixon appointed him vice president to replace Spiro Agnew, who had resigned after being accused of criminal acts.

Jimmy Carter and wife Rosalynn wave after his 1976
win over Gerald Ford. Carter won by only
fifty-seven electoral votes.

Not long after that, Nixon himself resigned as a result
of the Watergate scandal, and Ford became president.

Carter's popular-vote victory over Ford in 1976
was decisive—about 1,680,000 votes. The electoral
vote, however, was closer than in any election in over

fifty years. Carter won 297 electoral votes; Ford got 240. In Hawaii, Ford lost by fewer than 8,000 votes; in Mississippi, by fewer than 15,000; and in Ohio, by about 11,000. If Ford had carried these states, he would have been elected president, still trailing Carter by more than 1,000,000 votes.

It has been more than one hundred years since a popular winner failed to win the presidency. The possibility, however, will always exist. As long as the electoral college is in place, candidates running for president will have to consider not only how many votes they will win, but in which states those votes are cast.

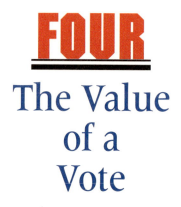

The Value
of a
Vote

Many Americans believe that every vote cast for president is of equal value. They may know that an electoral college exists and that all of their state's electoral votes go to the presidential candidate who gets the highest number of votes. Most people, however, are unaware that a vote cast in Idaho or Wyoming does not have the same value as a vote cast in California or New York. In fact, a vote in Wyoming can be said to be worth almost four times as much as a vote in California.

Many Americans do not realize that the "value of a vote" differs from state to state. In fact, votes cast in small states have a greater "value" than votes cast in more populous states.

The distribution of electoral votes
in the United States

Wyoming, with a population of 460,000, has three electoral votes—one for each of its two senators and one for its one member of the House of Representatives. Wyoming, therefore, has approximately one electoral vote for every 150,000 of its citizens. California, the state with the most electoral votes, is granted fifty-four electoral votes according to the same formula—one for each of its two senators and one for each of its fifty-two members of the House of Representatives. California's population is over 30 million. California, therefore, has one electoral vote for every 551,000 citizens. Thus, each vote cast in Wyoming is worth about 3.67 times as much as each vote cast in California.

Since no state can have fewer than three electoral votes, states with small populations, such as Wyoming, Alaska, and South Dakota, as well as Washington, D.C., seem to have a disproportionate influence in presidential elections. That is, voters in small states are granted a more powerful voice than their population size would indicate.

On the other hand, in different ways, the electoral college system favors large states with many electoral votes. In reality, there are fifty-one different presidential elections—one in each state and one in Wash-

ington, D.C. In order to get enough electoral votes to win the White House, candidates must run their fifty-one separate presidential campaigns with the electoral count clearly in mind. Although smaller states have a greater "vote value" per citizen than do the larger states, states with only a few electoral votes are given less priority than states with many electoral votes.

Presidential candidates map their campaign strategy accordingly by concentrating on winning states with many electoral votes. Some experts say that Richard Nixon lost the 1960 election to John F. Kennedy because he failed to concentrate on the states with the most electoral votes. During his campaigning, Nixon pledged to visit all fifty states, big and small. Meanwhile, Kennedy focused on a few, key states with large populations, such as Texas and Illinois. The results of the election were fascinating. The popular vote was one of the closest in history. The electoral vote, how-

Throughout the campaign, both sides closely track electoral vote counts. Returns are posted on the tally board at Kennedy campaign headquarters on election night in 1960. *Inset*: John F. Kennedy with running mate Lyndon B. Johnson

Nixon acknowledges applause in 1968 with his famous
two-handed victory sign. He went on to win the election
with less than 44 percent of the popular vote.

ever, showed Kennedy the unmistakable winner. If Nixon had concentrated on the large states as his opponent had, the outcome might have been different.

In some other presidential races, the electoral college system has distorted the wish of each voter. For example, in 1968, eight years after his devastatingly close popular-vote loss to Kennedy, Nixon ran against Hubert Humphrey, a Democrat, for the White House. The race included a third candidate, George Wallace, the governor of Alabama. Although he was a Democrat, Wallace ran as an independent who opposed new federal civil-rights laws.

Richard Nixon won the presidency with 301 electoral votes, 31 more than he needed. However, he received less than 44 percent of the popular vote. (Wallace carried five southern states, earned forty-six electoral votes, and won about 14 percent of the popular vote nationwide.) Thus, although the majority of Americans voted for other candidates, Nixon won the White House. In fact, nine other presidents in U.S. history have been elected with the support of less than 50 percent of American voters. Examples include Abraham Lincoln, Woodrow Wilson, and Harry S. Truman.

The 1992 election is the most recent instance in which a candidate won the White House without winning the majority of the popular vote. When Bill Clinton was elected president in 1992, he won a majority vote only in his home state of Arkansas and in Washington, D.C. (Remember a candidate need not capture a majority of a state's votes to win its presidential election and all of its electoral votes.) In every other state of the thirty-two he carried, Clinton received less than 50 percent of the vote. In a few states, he won the state's electoral votes with less than 40 percent of the vote.

Clearly, then, the way American presidents and vice presidents are chosen is not entirely democratic. The electoral college system does not always accurately reflect the will of the people, and there are many problems with the electoral process. Votes in different states have different values; votes in small states are proportionally worth more than votes in larger states. Conversely, the distribution of electoral votes forces candidates to focus on large states and overlook smaller states. And the winner-take-all system that works in most state presidential elections has its disadvantages: the winner receives all of the state's electoral votes, causing any votes for other candidates to be entirely meaningless. Lastly, the electoral system has even put popular-vote losers in the White House.

Why doesn't the United States simply elect its

Bill Clinton and Al Gore celebrate after their 1992 win.
Elected without a majority vote, Clinton joined presidents
Nixon, Truman, Wilson, and Lincoln.

president and vice president by a direct, popular vote? Wouldn't the nation be better served if the candidate who earned the most votes nationwide became president? And if no candidate won a majority vote, why not let the two candidates with the most votes face each other in a runoff election? After all, this process elects almost every other public official in the United States.

The pros and cons of the electoral college process have been debated widely. After more than two hundred years, the plan for presidential elections devised by the founders of the country inspires more debate than ever.

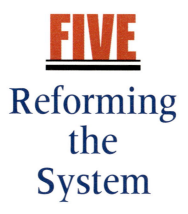

FIVE

Reforming the System

In the time that has passed since the Constitutional Convention of 1787 agreed upon the electoral college system, America has changed greatly. Today's voters, with access to media coverage of all kinds, are much better informed about candidates than voters of the past. Political parties have come to dominate politics in a way that the country's founders never imagined. Campaigning for president has become a multimillion-dollar endeavor. The union of states, which was fragile and new in 1787, is firmly established.

Learning about candidates and taking part in the political system is easier now than when the electoral college was created. For this reason among others, some say the electoral college has outlasted its usefulness.

Despite all these changes, the electoral system remains a part of the American political heritage. The United States cannot change the way it elects its presidents and vice presidents without first changing the U.S. Constitution itself. The only way to reform the electoral college system is to amend the Constitution. The nation's founders, however, purposely created a constitution that would be difficult to amend. The Constitution was to be a basic law, preserving certain timeless human rights and liberties.

However, it is possible to amend the Constitution. The process involves two steps. First, the U.S. Senate and House of Representatives must approve the amendment by a two-thirds majority vote. Second, the amendment must be approved by the legislatures of three-quarters, or thirty-eight, of the states. If only thirteen states were to object to a proposed constitutional amendment to do away with the electoral college, for example, the amendment would not be enacted.

In all likelihood, the smaller states would object to such an amendment. None of these states would gain influence or power from an amendment that did away with the electoral college. In fact, they would lose much of their electoral influence. A direct, popular vote in place of the electoral college system would diminish the "value" of the votes in the smaller states. Votes cast in states with small populations would no longer be worth three or four times as much as votes cast in states with larger populations.

We the People

We the People of the United States, in order to form a more perfect Union, establish Justice, insure domestic Tranquility, provide for the common defence, promote the general Welfare, and secure the Blessings of Liberty to ourselves and our Posterity, do ordain and establish this Constitution for the United States of America.

Article. I.

Section. 1. All legislative Powers herein granted shall be vested in a Congress of the United States, which shall consist of a Senate and House of Representatives.

Section. 2. The House of Representatives shall be composed of Members chosen every second Year by the People of the several States, and the Electors in each State shall have the Qualifications requisite for Electors of the most numerous Branch of the State Legislature.

No Person shall be a Representative who shall not have attained to the Age of twenty five Years, and been seven Years a Citizen of the United States, and who shall not, when elected, be an Inhabitant of that State in which he shall be chosen.

Representatives and direct Taxes shall be apportioned among the several States which may be included within this Union, according to their respective Numbers, which shall be determined by adding to the whole Number of free Persons, including those bound to Service for a Term of Years, and excluding Indians not taxed, three fifths of all other Persons. The actual Enumeration shall be made within three Years after the first Meeting of the Congress of the United States, and within every subsequent Term of ten Years, in such Manner as they shall by Law direct. The Number of Representatives shall not exceed one for every thirty Thousand, but each State shall have at Least one Representative; and until such enumeration shall be made, the State of New Hampshire shall be entitled to chuse three, Massachusetts eight, Rhode Island and Providence Plantations one, Connecticut five, New York six, New Jersey four, Pennsylvania eight, Delaware one, Maryland six, Virginia ten, North Carolina five, South Carolina five, and Georgia three.

When vacancies happen in the Representation from any State, the Executive Authority thereof shall issue Writs of Election to fill such Vacancies.

The House of Representatives shall chuse their Speaker and other Officers; and shall have the sole Power of Impeachment.

Section. 3. The Senate of the United States shall be composed of two Senators from each State, chosen by the Legislature thereof, for six Years; and each Senator shall have one Vote.

Immediately after they shall be assembled in Consequence of the first Election, they shall be divided as equally as may be into three Classes. The Seats of the Senators of the first Class shall be vacated at the Expiration of the second Year, of the second Class at the Expiration of the fourth Year, and of the third Class at the Expiration of the sixth Year, so that one third may be chosen every second Year; and if Vacancies happen by Resignation, or otherwise, during the Recess of the Legislature of any State, the Executive thereof may make temporary Appointments until the next Meeting of the Legislature, which shall then fill such Vacancies.

No Person shall be a Senator who shall not have attained to the Age of thirty Years, and been nine Years a Citizen of the United States, and who shall not, when elected, be an Inhabitant of that State for which he shall be chosen.

The Vice President of the United States shall be President of the Senate, but shall have no Vote, unless they be equally divided.

The Senate shall chuse their other Officers, and also a President pro tempore, in the Absence of the Vice President, or when he shall exercise the Office of President of the United States.

The Senate shall have the sole Power to try all Impeachments. When sitting for that Purpose, they shall be on Oath or Affirmation. When the President of the United States is tried, the Chief Justice shall preside: And no Person shall be convicted without the Concurrence of two thirds of the Members present.

Judgment in Cases of Impeachment shall not extend further than to removal from Office, and disqualification to hold and enjoy any Office of honor, Trust or Profit under the United States: but the Party convicted shall nevertheless be liable and subject to Indictment, Trial, Judgment and Punishment, according to Law.

Section. 4. The Times, Places and Manner of holding Elections for Senators and Representatives, shall be prescribed in each State by the Legislature thereof; but the Congress may at any time by Law make or alter such Regulations, except as to the Places of chusing Senators.

The Congress shall assemble at least once in every Year, and such Meeting shall be on the first Monday in December, unless they shall by Law appoint a different Day.

Section. 5. Each House shall be the Judge of the Elections, Returns and Qualifications of its own Members, and a Majority of each shall constitute a Quorum to do Business; but a smaller Number may adjourn from day to day, and may be authorized to compel the Attendance of absent Members, in such Manner, and under such Penalties as each House may provide.

Each House may determine the Rules of its Proceedings, punish its Members for disorderly Behaviour, and, with the Concurrence of two thirds, expel a Member.

Each House shall keep a Journal of its Proceedings, and from time to time publish the same, excepting such Parts as may in their Judgment require Secrecy; and the Yeas and Nays of the Members of either House on any question shall, at the Desire of one fifth of those Present, be entered on the Journal.

Neither House, during the Session of Congress, shall, without the Consent of the other, adjourn for more than three days, nor to any other Place than that in which the two Houses shall be sitting.

Section. 6. The Senators and Representatives shall receive a Compensation for their Services, to be ascertained by Law, and paid out of the Treasury of the United States. They shall in all Cases, except Treason, Felony and Breach of the Peace, be privileged from Arrest during their Attendance at the Session of their respective Houses, and in going to and returning from the same; and for any Speech or Debate in either House, they shall not be questioned in any other Place.

No Senator or Representative shall, during the Time for which he was elected, be appointed to any civil Office under the Authority of the United States, which shall have been created, or the Emoluments whereof shall have been encreased during such time; and no Person holding any Office under the United States, shall be a Member of either House during his Continuance in Office.

Section. 7. All Bills for raising Revenue shall originate in the House of Representatives; but the Senate may propose or concur with Amendments as on other Bills.

Every Bill which shall have passed the House of Representatives and the Senate, shall, before it become a Law, be presented to the President of the

There is another way that the electoral system could be altered. States could drop the winner-take-all system and permit candidates to win a portion of their state's total electors. Although most states use the winner-take-all system, the Constitution allows state legislatures to appoint electors however they choose. Maine and Nebraska already have recognized and adopted this alternative, and in recent years, a number of states have considered such proposals for "proportional representation" among the electors. Proportional representation means dividing a state's electors among the candidates to match the proportion of votes they received in the election.

Distributing a state's electoral votes to many different candidates, however, would weaken that state's influence and power. California's fifty-four electoral votes, for example, are a huge prize for any candidate. That prize is why candidates campaign so

The U.S. Constitution is a living document that can be changed with the times. The last amendment, passed in 1992, prohibits midterm pay raises for members of Congress.

The electoral college has changed little from its creation in 1787. The official count of electoral votes cast in the individual state capitals still takes place in Congress.

hard in California and in the other states that have many electoral college votes. If the electoral votes of these populous states could be divided among the candidates, those states would receive less attention from the candidates than they currently do.

The United States will most probably retain the electoral college as it is. The smaller states are unlikely to approve a constitutional amendment to provide for national, "one person, one vote" elections. The shift of the nation's current balance of electoral power would be too dramatic. Most states are also unlikely to abandon the winner-take-all system of allocating electors. Proportional distribution of electors carries with it the uncertainties of an independent, third-party winner. And state legislatures, dominated by the Democratic and Republican parties, are unlikely to support any plan that minimizes party influences on presidential elections.

If the nation were ever to experience another election that sent a candidate to the White House without having won the popular election, support for reform might increase. The delegates to the Constitutional Convention of 1787 created the electoral college because they thought it was the best way to satisfy the concerns of all states—large and small—

and to provide for a president elected by ordinary Americans. When the current electoral system fails to produce strong leaders, the time for change will have arrived. For now, the electoral college continues to be one of the most controversial and misunderstood parts of the U.S. political system.

GLOSSARY

Activist—a person who works on behalf of a cause or political party

Bloc—a group united to support a common cause

Elector—one of several representatives chosen by the voters of each state to elect the president and vice president

Electoral college—the body of electors chosen by voters from each state to elect the president and vice president

Electoral votes—the votes a candidate wins from the electoral college

Majority—a number of votes cast for a candidate that equals more than 50 percent of the total vote in an election

Minority—a number of votes less than is needed for control

Plurality—a number of votes cast for a candidate that equals 50 percent or less of the total vote but more than that received by any other candidate in an election

Popular vote—the total votes cast by individual voters for candidates in a given election

Quorum—the minimum number of legislators that must be present to enact a law or to conduct other official business

Runoff election—a follow-up election between the two highest vote-getters that takes place when an election has no majority-vote winner

Slate—a list of candidates

FOR FURTHER READING

Blassingame, Wyatt. *The Look-It-Up Book of Presidents*. New York: Random House, 1990.

Feinberg, Barbara Silberdick. *Words in the News: A Student's Dictionary of American Government and Politics*. New York: Franklin Watts, 1993.

Hanneman, Tamara. *Election Book: People Pick a President.* New York: Scholastic, 1992.

Harvey, Miles. *Presidential Elections.* Chicago: Childrens Press, 1995.

Pious, Richard M. *The Presidency.* Englewood Cliffs, N.J.: Silver Burdett Press, 1991.

Raber, Thomas R. *Election Night.* Minneapolis: Lerner Publications, 1988.

———. *Presidential Campaign.* Minneapolis: Lerner Publications, 1988.

Samuels, Cythnia K. *It's a Free Country! A Young Person's Guide to Politics and Elections.* New York: Atheneum, 1988.

Sullivan, George. *Campaigns and Elections.* Morristown, N.J.: Silver Burdett Press, 1991.

———. *Choosing the Candidates.* Morristown, N.J.: Silver Burdett Press, 1991.

INDEX

ABOUT THE AUTHOR

CHRISTOPHER HENRY is a New York attorney in private practice. He has written several books for children, including *Ruth Bader Ginsburg* and *Sandra Day O'Connor* for Franklin Watts. Mr. Henry is the author of two other First Books about the American political process: *Presidential Conventions* and *Presidential Elections*.

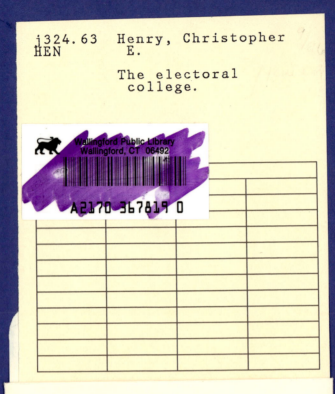